# WHAT PLANET

**Miriam Gamble** was born in Brussels in 1980 and grew up in Belfast. She studied at Oxford and at Queen's University Belfast, where she completed a PhD in contemporary British and Irish poetry. She won an Eric Gregory Award in 2007, and the Ireland Chair of Poetry Bursary Award in 2010. Her pamphlet, *This Man's Town*, was published by tall-lighthouse in 2007. She has published three book-length collections with Bloodaxe: her debut, *The Squirrels Are Dead* (2010), winner of a Somerset Maugham Award in 2011, *Pirate Music* (2014), and *What Planet* (2019). She lectures in creative writing at Edinburgh University.

# MIRIAM GAMBLE

# What Planet

## BLOODAXE BOOKS

ISBN: 978 1 78037 484 0

First published 2019 by
Bloodaxe Books Ltd,
Eastburn,
South Park,
Hexham,
Northumberland NE46 1BS,


**www.bloodaxebooks.com**
For further information about Bloodaxe titles
please visit our website and join our mailing list
or write to the above address for a catalogue

Supported using public funding by
**ARTS COUNCIL
ENGLAND**

Cover design: Neil Astley & Pamela Robertson-Pearce.


Printed in Great Britain by Bell & Bain Limited, Glasgow, Scotland, on
acid-free paper sourced from mills with FSC chain of custody certification.

*For my parents*

# ACKNOWLEDGEMENTS

Thanks are due to the editors of the following magazines and anthologies, where some of these poems, or versions of these poems, first appeared: *Alice: Ekphrasis at the British Library* (Joy Lane Publishing, 2016), *The Café Review, The Compass, The Dark Horse, Female Lines: New Writing by Women from Northern Ireland* (New Island, 2017), *The Irish Review, Poetry* (Chicago), *Poetry Ireland Review, The Tangerine, Umbrellas of Edinburgh* (Freight Books, 2016), *The Undertow Review* and *Virginia Quarterly Review*.

'Feria de Málaga' was commissioned by Writers' Centre Norwich as part of the 'Crossing Borders' series for the 2017 International Literature Showcase. 'Time Ball' appeared on the Edinburgh City Council Website through city makar Christine de Luca's 'Edinburgh Unsung' project. 'The Canal at Fountainbridge', 'Moths' and 'IndyRef, 2014' converse with and originally featured alongside poems by Nerys Williams in the collaborative pamphlet *City of Two Suns* (Irish Writers' Centre, 2016). 'Betty Staff's' came second in the 2015 Strokestown International Poetry Prize. My especial thanks go to The Shore Poets for giving me the 2018 Mark Ogle Memorial Award ('Feldspar' responds to Mark's poem 'Coastal Walk: Islay'), and to Neil Astley, Alan Gillis and Peter Mackay for offering invaluable advice on the poems.

# CONTENTS

*If this is not the truth, it is also not a lie*

CLAUDIA RANKINE

## The Landing Window Is Unspeakable

There's a turn in the stairs beyond which,
in the darkness, you are terrified to go –
the realm of the creaking life which somehow carries on
when everyone is out cold and unable to witness it.

There's a mind-made barrier at the door
of your parents' room: their sleeping frightens you,
the heavy breath, the still, recumbent forms.

You've been ferried back from light-drenched places,
in coaches, the customary glare
of the mint-green bathroom trebled in intensity,
like it sucked in pigment while you were gone.

Then woken foxed by the dimensions of the house
you've lived your whole conscious life in.
The recurrent dream of a cat walking a wall,
a provisional touching your father's hair.

# The Oak That Was Not There

The oak that was not there was not there
and the sands went walking under the sea.

The clocks went forward, the clocks went back.
Someone lost their temper with me.

From a hillock, we looked on as water
swept its grey silk garment through the estuary.

The clocks went forward, the clocks went back.
The penitent, down on his knees, begged

for the honey of forgiveness from a round god whose
presence we had proven.

The clocks went forward, the clocks went back;
there was no response. But we must act responsibly!

said our grave leader as the flowers of the machair
grew scissor faces. On their faces,

the hands of the second went chop, chop, chop;
the digitalis ate a mink. To think,

one murmured, that it should come down to this.
Another nodded: I consent there is something wrong –

as the blown-glass nimbi angled and clinked
and the clocks went back and forwards, back and forwards –

Where is the oak, for one thing? Where is the blasted oak?
And the round god fell from the sky like a fish.

# Time Ball

When it falls
for the last time, thudding
through the mechanisms geared to
contain it and the last shot fires, the last
ship calibrates its sundry instruments, is pinned
one final time by time onto the wall, it will keep
on falling, thrusting through the mechanisms geared
to contain it; though the clocks still tick in the centre
of the city it will cannon through the crust into the
magma – and the clocks still ticking in the centre
with the neat hands and the mark of the maker
will tick for no one, for eight full days
express like metronomes the bare
bones of a score

## Odradek Returns

Why? And indeed,
you may well ask the question.
It can hardly be said that here
is as good as anywhere.

I acknowledge that I don't
much kindle to it –
the humourlessness, for example,
the speech like little silver bells.
And it has no claim upon me.

At heart, I would say
I'm a creature of pines and rivers,
but there are no pines or rivers.
At heart, I would say
I am certain of what I want –
and it doesn't look like this.

Dead dogs and kaleidoscopes,
am I of a piece
with this neutered city?
What is it that I plan
on achieving here, exactly?

They say I have the look
of a fragment but display no seam.
No one is more confused than me
as to what is meant by it.

# Wonderland

It came to me of a sudden that my neighbour was a threat to peace, security, the nation. Previously I had had no sense of this but I knew it to be true so I set about letting the people know who should know and I must say it was a source of pride when, on the basis of my information, he was carried away for questioning, his face blank as a moon.

I dream sometimes that my neighbour is a nut in a cluster of nuts hanging on a tree. They're out of reach and beautiful, glinting in the sun, and my dream-self wants to grab one. I don't know what it means; but did I say that the Queen called, afterwards, to offer her congratulations? I said to her, Your Majesty (and here I grew feet taller than my normal stature), what you see is what you get, and I am a personage who knows what he sees. She liked that, though – the strangest thing – she complained of snow when one felt quite clearly it was balmy and the depths of summer: flowers blossoming to the waist, bees whipping the pollen into sugared combs.

# Amethyst

When you dropped to the floor and were not able to get up,
it would have been the end of you; nobody, not even I
would have been able to help; nothing could be done for you,
    no hand
would assist you, no loving shoulder guide you to a bed
and prop you up, thumb smooth the hair from your brow. Your
    mind

is the beautiful shock whose name means 'not intoxicated';
in your skull, so many chambers glittering with light, so many
refractory gemstones. They would have smashed it
like a pomegranate, they would have trampled the rich seeds,
all your islands, into the mouthless dirt. That lightning

that flickers in your not-right spine would have charged itself,
and would have brought you to the ground; you would have
    hunched like a crab
in the inspection lines. And from my steel-rope body,
I would have witnessed your excruciating bid to straighten – for,
heaven help me, nothing ails my form – as the monsters hooked
    you out.

# Coda

When I made it back to the burnt amphitheatre
you were sitting with your chin in your hands,
your elbows on your knees, just like I'd left you
before the city went on fire,
before I ran whatever message I'd to get.
I knew you gone from the moment
I saw flames ripping through the streets like tinder.
But you were graspable. Blood weighted your tread.

I said, 'I hunkered in the sea, did you not go to the sea?'
'I have my pride,' you said. And then, 'I don't feel different at all.'
I put my hand on your knee I touched my lips
to your heavy head. '*Why* could you not have done it?'
I asked pointlessly. Fire made bright your features.
We sat on, quiet now, as though we were in bed,
each touching the other every passing while.

# Feria de Málaga

Fuck knows what it's all about but if you really want to drink Cartojal a beaded bag ought to be purchased for our wits given how everybody here's like their inner head fell off. Even at the best of times, and it's hardly the best of times, someone is as apt as not, you know it, to un-lever the stone under which we're hunkered for the purposes of building a low wall or hiding stuff. They won't mean to kill us, they'll only want to sleep when it's too cold to sleep without a wind-deflecting wall, or to bury things they covet and have nicked from a neighbour such as say, perhaps, a wife, a jammy roll, a frame like a resplendent crust. But in the way we're in the way and love, that's life in a universe of cold calculation so you keep your wits about you and you don't drink Cartojal or potions of its ilk saving you must, as for example now.

# Leòdhasach

The song of your faithful is like life
rolled whimpering through a mangle, backwards.

Your trees are hair whipped
stiff behind a ghoul that's only head.

Instead of greenery you have stripped-
backery; instead of mammals, the mutant cleg.

On the thin road into the level dark
two taxis angle frail antennae.

Here is the sky, here is the sky
heavier on my head than I want to know it,

licking the flesh from my temples as we walk
like my supple skin were sorbet.

Here the bog which, though you don't
know the names for anything, you read

in the leap before you land and here am I, hip
snapped like a fowl's, in its brackish consommé.

# The Holy Host in Spanish Art

Here, the carpets of heaven sink lower
than they do in other places.
At least once daily a foot will obtrude
like that of an upstairs neighbour
in a cheaply plastered flat,
and there are times you can barely
raise your body to its full height,
the kitchen suddenly quaintly Victorian.

Bang your pots and pans – they won't
back off, and when you fill the kettle
they'll have laced the water, such
that when that night you visit the baths
you grab the masseuse round the waist,
thinking she is some kind of chimera,
as her hands unmould the reefs of panic
in your neck, in your skull, spine, shoulders,
and an angry conger eel exits its haunt.

## Gutties

On this shoe you have centred all your hopes
of becoming a finished person: you tie it onto you and wait
for the magic to occur.
You've perceived how, in the playground lines,
it heat-seals the tips of other children, the exclamatory stroke
that signals an artwork; how it holds them like a cup holds juice.
And now you tie it onto you, you admire
the clean white leather with the emerald flashes,
imitation Adidas out of Dunnes but
its credentials are neither here nor there;
it is the only hope for you
and you tie it on tightly though, admittedly, even in the shop,
the alchemy drains out of it inverse to your clammy presence –
with which desire and gain have nothing to do.

## Alchemist

Later he will dress for dinner, though for now
he is embarrassed that the only thing he has to offer is the
    Lucozade
we brought, though by now he has forgotten that we brought it
if in fact he ever realised that we had. In his hands,
it's a bottle of despicable stuff he's somehow in possession of –
though God knows what, he mulls, compelled him to avail of it
or compelled the hired help to set it out. We sit
on with him into the cocktail hour, drinking the inferior red
out of crystal glasses; this is the time
for Gin and Tonics, always was, and again he laments of the
    butler's taste.
You cannot get, he says to us, the staff these days;
even when you are offering good money
there is nothing there but riff raff to be bought.
Crisp, starchy, the dress shirt he will wear to dinner
when he goes with the other men to the club
to talk about the war and the next good outing to be
ghosts the chair; beneath it are his spats. There's a gramophone
singing in the corner, and if you listen closely you can hear
the planes already rising heavily from German runways
even though there are many hours until night.

# Betty Staff's

In retrospect it turns out that her bouncer was like an octopus,
nimbling across the floor to take his fill from the bar,
perched back sweetly at his post
before a body would think to look. It's the 1950s,
so she doesn't have cameras on the door or on the dance floor.
He flashes his teeth, parades the tart liquor on his breath

to the queue of nice specimens from the Shankill who, in a breath,
will shift their coloration like mimic octopuses,
stepping out neatly and daintily in pairs across the floor,
picking out from the clutch of men at the bar,
with expert eyes, the silver-haired foxes in their fifties
who'll keep them in drink, and the young bucks with whom they'll
        take up post

for the slower numbers. His back straight as a post,
Betty's partner steers her through a tango, while the punters catch
        their breath.
She was a wan child when she came here to work, but by the 1950s
Betty's living the life: she's like something out of *Octopussy*
or some such yet-to-be-invented model for glamour, and there seems
        no bar
to her success, though mastery of the dance floor

isn't everything, and there is space on Betty Staff's floor
like you wouldn't want, no matter the scores of bills she posts
in the city's theatres and tea-shops, the high-end hotel bars.
Betty's a snob, they say, under their breath.
When you go out dancing you want to go octopus,
and there's no jiving at Betty's, and this is the 1950s

and where else can you not go jiving in the 1950s...
Who does the stiff bitch think she is? Would it floor
Betty if she knew this? Would it sour her puss
to know that her dance hall is the hall of last resort for the post-
pub heading-for-the-swinging-60s crowds? Put to it, an octopus
  can hold its breath
for thirty minutes out of water, can navigate a bar

of land as expertly as Betty Staff holds herself at the barre.
Things won't always be like they are in the 1950s,
though Betty's already learned to hold her breath
by the 50s, not that you'd know to watch her move across the floor.
Betty believes in appearances, she knows how to keep her post.
At home, her husband flails like an octopus –

more than once he will knock her to the floor, and free of breath.
But to the jewel-clad notion of the post-war 1950s,
Betty will play the mother octopus – *Lengthen your neck. Die nacht
ist wunderbar –*

in ever more deadly earnest.

# Feldspar

We drew level with her on the roundabout
in the Citroën with the flash suspension,
or what was then the flash suspension;
observing her bowed body, two
plastic bags of supermarket shopping
in her hands, the pained
labour of her gait, you cursed,
and cursed once more your father's stubbornness,
akin to madness, and motioned mine
to stop the car – *What planet*
*is he living on that he can think*
*there's nothing wrong with her?!!!*

– And as the dusty rings of fantasy
swirled around the gas giant
of your father's head,
the liquor round his glass,
and he stretched his long legs
from the comfort of the sitting room sofa
and adjusted his bulk
in the leather, impressed a form
like to a hare's, we sat
in the Citroën's revolutionary
technology as though
in a dinghy and you lifted from her hands
the thin ply polythene which weighed
nothing at all –

       – Though for her,
to carry it was like
throwing a sack of kittens
in the river, her whole
being weighted down,

manufacturing rock
in insidious crystal chains
that densened in the dark
heat of her core.

She, the one-time
queen of posture. For a second,
she straightened like she might
offer to dance.

# Incident Report

He's walking like he's legged
with blades of scissors –
one sticky hinge at the navel.
Into the road, then out again,
into the road, then out.

The big boom of the radio,
if his ears could smell,
would be raw gas, odourless.
In my – veering – in my sky
blue walnut shell, I pass.

When they come, will the cops
find any person matching up
to my description? If I drove
right into him, would two
bodies collide? All the journey

I'm tortured by the notion
that he must, *must* have been killed,
stalking crazy in the road like that.
But nothing makes the news
and no one follows up my call.

## The Wits

commence thrusting out of my chin.
Monthly, the beautician snaps
strings together; between,
I remove rogue elements myself
with a purpose-built tool

or else I angle scissors, strim
the scarecrow fingers of the consciousness
coiled like a whip against me,
sad creature havocking
at its own proportionate skin.

# Oils of Sculptors Working

Not monumental undertakings
but scions of self,
a foot or so in height;
small corners of imagination,
clay-cleft, realised
as the painter stood
dabbing the shadows in.

Buckshot eyes pin the sculptor
like a temporary god
to the heavens
of the ill-lit studio;
the wings are wet, hesitant,
ready to be fired –
stray thoughts hardening
into brittle, bewildered forms.

# Crane Fly

The sullen gait of the spider,
the body of the one fly
flicking into life, entangled in web,
affixed to the other,
in which no message travels

The tussle with the abdomens
in the low beam, the dead form
dropping away through the decking
as through a great crevasse,
the tussle with the legs, the wings
more fragile than a liquid's surface

As though in a narrative
the actual success of the operation,
the pinioning with kitchen roll
of the balled web, two legs loosed
like the hairs from a beet

but the creature flying, definitively flying,
chaotically propelled over the fence
and resuming balance, the spider's
impassive looking on
from the hanks of its shredded tool

# Parotia Displaying in a Forest Clearing

Say, rather, that his dancing is demonic, that he invokes
terrible gods, or, as D'Albertis put it as he held the first
specimen, musters an invisible foe. Say
that the brown bird looking on gives audience
only in the sense that Commodus gave audience, or as the listener
to an overheard voice. Call the brown one neither he
nor she, do not factor attention in
to the solemn dancing; disregard the facts you know
are pertinent to the raised circlet of pseudo-wing,
the wedding headgear wires.
                This defrocked cleric
hiking skirts and jigging to the song Satanic
– or even better, an un-defrocked one – say
he never meant anyone to see; that he enacts his little rite
in call and response to the music
of eternal darkness; above all else, insist
it is a private ecstasy. That he's crazy on laudanum.
That he doesn't know himself,
or knows himself for the first time.
That he hates his parishioners with a village hate
and seeks to bring pestilence down upon their heads.

                Or if it must be sex
let it be onanism, pleasurable, pointless and ornate.
Under the light of a supermoon
let the watcher make haste to the village hall.

# Plume

Meadowsweet heads just out of bed and plotting like the bitch out of *Dangerous Liaisons* for – something. Or perhaps, like Mozart, they're composing in those creamy wigs – that's why they're so plump and plumy, yet at the same time otherworldly. Those heads like natural cotton candy, the shape of Scotland, the colour of fat gathered in the top of old-school milk bottles, the fat birds would filch before you took it in, those heads are packed with notes, with symphonies, and with no means of getting them down onto paper to be played in undying perpetuity by orchestras and orchestras, the heads grow bigger by the day, perhaps even the hour, until they are truly fit to explode: the slim scarlet necks can barely hold them up, that they do is an engineering miracle.

# Girl with Book and Rubber Bands

She has a book and she's attached it
to a string of rubber bands
knotted like you used to do for playing inside-outside,
or like you'd make a makeshift punchball.

Bam! The book flies into the air
and the people in the stalled cars turn to see it.

*Don't stare!* our inner mothers warn.

But we have never seen a girl
on a crisp autumn's day
operating a paperback like a missile
with assorted rubber bands.

What in God's name's got into her head?

And, with our handbrakes on,
with our four-strokes
ticking over, we watch transfixed
as it buckets through the air.

A car nudges into another car, and no one cares;
the news is like a grim stuck record,
but there is this girl
sending out and reeling in a book on a rubber leash.

Tomorrow she will be a brat – the type
to ask you in the street
if you're some kind of a dick bastard,
to simper Oh-My-God would you *look* at her *hair*?

But today she is magnificent, today
we watch her and we like the cut of her jib more than
anything
as she cackles and flexes,
as she sends the book cantering through the air

for the solo delectation of her mate, who sits
on the paving stones doubled up with screaming laughter.
Their bags decorate a branch.
Their shoes are nowhere to be seen.

# Bloater

Not being a carnivore you never look like you ate an anvil, like something large and supremely indigestible, with hooves, with fine-boned shins and flicking ears, eyes clogging with the goo of your saliva, is wodged in your whistle which, if prised wide open, would reveal limbs going in as first those limbs came out, perhaps no more than several weeks ago, from someone else's orifice, sheathed lightly in a sac. There are not in your innards oiled tufts accumulating in the corners, the bends and diversions of your tracts, nor things stored darkly for disintegration live or dead, for creeping acid breakdown. None of these: instead, you appear all summer as though someone had inserted a pump up your slathered sphincter of the kind used for inflating lilos, thigh-twanging furniture, paddling pools, and pressed, and pressed, and pressed till your sleek hide apes a cartoon bomb, of which your tail, plaited for travel, forms the unlit fuse.

# Enkidu's Worm

has siphoned from the brain of the cherished one a dish
delectable enough one might speak of caviar
or truffles as procured for the bearers of elite
coin pressed in London. As with these,
a little goes a long way in a single go
so the worm heads down the furry flume
of the nostril making fine use of the cilia
as a form of rigging. It wouldn't eat down to the bone
even had it bulk to afford it for the worm
like all wild gatherings of matter keeps its shape, and knows
when necessity is sated and respects that borderline.
To the great king and warrior it nods a civic 'hello'
then picks out ably its passage from the mouth
of the crater down the sloped sides of the pimpling scree.

## Mare at Large

The mare
has lifted into the sky, has cleared the hedge
and breached the next farm along.
All afternoon she will gallop freely
with her tail over her back;
she isn't minded to be caught.

She has jumped, and she will gallop –
the mare who, finding your finger in her jaws,
will press the bone
and look at you
and stop.

A mare
is not a river,
is not a child jumping hedges
from the window of a train –
gather and reach, gather and reach,
jump the houses, the factories and everything:
what is visible is jumpable, so long
as the striding's right.

A mare
is not a river. She will tire,
will take into her foam-slashed mouth
a carrot like a finger,
she will be caught.

But still, the mare has jumped the hedge
and breached the next farm along.
She has galloped all afternoon,
flags
flaunting in the wind.
This cannot be taken away from her.

# Credentials

The mother still holds sway as the only thing
ever to get the better of the horse
who's run you back and forth
with a squared jaw over the field breaks
of all these years, sweating, swearing.

It spent the night in the hay rack once
batting your woman in the face
should she approach – out
went the soft feeler of nose and out
went the armoured foot of the canny feline

which in its head framed the rapport
between dried fodder taken in
and deliberated by the jaws of the mare
and loss of the comfortable bed
it had finely happened on as it passed,

intent on dinner, so it hit her in the face
all night and retained the sweet
mattress of the hay oh felina triumphant
and when it fell pregnant you declared
full heartily I want me one of them.

## Siete Lagunas

In the night
you huddle to stay alive in the night
the fine-spun faces of the foxes exit holes
in the fabric of the mountain and apprise themselves
what's what        What has the sky
caught in its net has it dogs
with it has it dogs with it is there tin
cast round it and the bag that secures it is it edible
can it be burrowed through is it vegetal
is it fatty        Fatty's best, crystalled or cured
Off in a caravan of foxes if it honks
flesh if it smacks sugar should it have the juicy fizz
of the garden don't bother        Said, don't bother

When light comes up
on the thinly knotted hoop the embroidery
& particoloured wares of the one
night scavengers be gone        ascend
rock faces sprinkle greenery hot blood
focused on the freight        Have it in the mouth
in the belly in the back
bone of the tapestry snore-still or rolling in play
observe how the oily saucisson fletches your brush,
your intellect, with matter silken,
how your claws flash silver silver grey,
lengthening before your very eyes like dream escarpments
in the gloom in the spatter of squinnied rays

# Kitten

Bringing him home in the car, a handcup's white
spatter of fur in a carry box the scale
of the cavernous blue to Jonah, you thought him dead
of a heart attack and halted to check.
In what you remember as the dark but
can't have been given it was summer,
round eyes met your hazel stare. The throat
withheld its music; wary as mussels,
the lungs creaked on their fragile string.
Your face against the grid, blunt as a shark.

## Marine Snow

The memory of sun, it is what they subsist upon
down where the jaws snap blindly
at whatever passes, where drifter is a meaningless term

and to hunt is to proffer teeth and tongue
and ghost-lit lantern
into a sea like liquid wind,
without prior compass
of the way the wind is blowing.

Should they be gifted with a corpse
whose half-spoilt flesh holds distillate
eternal summers
spent glittering in the euphotic zone,
they will give gross thanks and, in their way, be holy.

In the cartography of sea,
they are kin not to dragons nor the *Stella Maris*
but to your own bright band –

yes, you there, eating your sunlight second hand
from a long-gone grocery display,
drinking it from the guts of lazy lemons.

# The Canal at Fountainbridge

The water doesn't flow one way or the other
of its own imperative, but takes direction
from the wind; it turns back
on itself when it counters the lock,
peppered moth cut loose
from the products of industry.
At night, the swans spin on the decks
of its currents, and sieve, sleep, sieve,
light bulk knocking the rim like bathtub toys.

*   *   *

On a Sunday that reflects,
by the Classical process
of association, your last summer
as a girl – sun-bleached
silences, the trekking business
gone out of business
without ever admitting as much –
a man comes kilter to the grass
and the newly dug beds
by the stacked apartments,
head down and on his knees,
howling, digging.
You watch him from behind the glass
of a life going forwards, pretend
that you haven't seen him.
Men gather in a clutch;
he takes the town-wards path.

*   *   *

Here is ecology, here is the furtherance
of education, bright school climbing the sky,

its every out-facing surface a mirror.
Here are the Spanish boys drumming up

lonely salsas, a twirling glitter-ball, twigs
rubbed in the night. Here is the scurf

of the past, the clean scalp of the future.
Here is a landscape like the head

of an orator, meticulously shuffling
through its show of slides –

what is to be kept, and what forgotten,
and in what order. Here is health,

affixed to the careful management
of those weeping borders.

And here your own small past,
abstracted from it in a box
others will smash and squeeze.

# Gardyloo

*(to Andrew Chesney, the last inhabitant of Mary King's Close)*


Shit surfaced outside our flat last week
– Easter holidays, what's to be done? –
and I thought of you, proud
on your modern indoor throne,
the door flung open so that all could see you.
Shit scrolling down the street to the Nor' Loch
at seven and, *le soir*, at ten. On iced shit,
treacherously, people slipping forwards.

Forwards to the future, to me
with the toe of my boot going *What is that?*
*AH JESUS!!* mincing down the road
like my whole self's coated in miasmas,
my partner begging *Would you drop it?*
Ten o'clock on a Friday night and shit
on the public pavement by our window.
Andrex bloomed from the exploded drain like stars,

like subterranean flowers or the delicate
caparison of folks long sealed and stoppered,
douked into a rancid skin it took ten
minutes for your head to sink beneath,
all property repurposed by the town.
Hanging for men; for women a sick,
slow sputter in the pleasure gardens,
the guide's pun withering: *A crappy way to go.*

At the eye of the compulsory purchase shit
storm you, adamant but beaten, the street's
noise silenced and your gem, your dunny,
abandoned to the arsenic-covered walls.

*Well, fine*, I hear you say, and at ten o'clock,
with the St Giles tipping order, you cast
this tickertape, these shredded documents, this –
on the Athens of the North's sumptuous grey.

# Little Monument: Se Vende

Maybe it's the heat, or the sherry
from the ill-fated lunchtime "tour" of the bodega –
six glasses in half an hour between two of us,
as obligatory as they were deadly –
but when we get to the site
of the Museo del Mar Caracoles;
when we find the hand-painted sign
impishly emblazoned over someone else's,
and pendent at above head height;
when we see the empty apartment that,
if it signals anything, the sign addresses,
and, knowing before we even ask, when we ask
at the basket shop further down the street
and the woman makes a gesture with her hands;
when she puts so delicately her palms together,
and holds them up against her cheek,
and that's that, and we go back into the sun,
I pause to take a photograph
of the crude sign, a photograph
of the swagsick apartment; I have never felt
more like weeping for anyone.

# In Memoriam Your Stuff

At first my father tried to sort it through; diligent
in your front room as you lay in hospital,
he worked decades-old issues of the *Radio Times* loose
like a mother teasing out knots with a comb.
Returned to me on your death
were the objects I had bought for you:
a stone camel from Pakistan, a blown-glass cat.

He tried to winnow through it all like that,
to formalise the teeth of time
in a recognisable pattern, such that a crystallised pear
was distinguishable from a lump of gold. But you
did not seem to want your history told
and in the end it went en masse
down to the dump. You engineered it so,

who snuck warmth from the whisky of chaos,
who prized without hierarchy every thing.

# Urn

As the fluid thrusts into the vein
the whole gallimaufry seems to suck
into the vacuum, the syringe
goes fat with it the plunger settles to
like a rewound video the lot is nothinged

I have never let into my poems life's
rich jumble I am tough
too true I was anorexic who
wants to hear it here is world made metaphor
words like a hummingbird's bill
siphoning the inner nectar

They weigh nothing if you blinked
you would miss them they are like
blown ashes on the wind
on which I won't scatter you
I keep you for myself in a small
sealed vessel, because it is all I've got

# Handwriting

Now, when things come bearing it,
a hand you recognise
for its spindle or solidity,
which used to scribble notes
on the back of un-
opened statements cluttering your sideboard,
the universe fumbles a beat:

it exists, is still being fashioned;
the Basildon Bond pad
with the ruled guide sheet
continues to be stowed
in the head-high cabinet;
envelopes are being purchased, a fist
curled round a pen and words sent

winging from the nucleus to here.
The sight of it sends rogue
pulses to your inner ear.
There's something to it of the cormorant's
glaringly alive self planked
on the concrete by an urban towpath,
extending its wings with the luminosity

of a heart attack: you glimpse a pale-inked letter
working itself loose from the clutter
on a table-top that's yet to be;
yourself, in a room you at once
know and don't know, suddenly short of air,
startling at the cheery pop of toast.
Within it is, already, its creeping memory –

this botched signal that is like itself
knuckled with growths.

# Wormhole, Westlink

*(for my father)*

You hold the arrow in your hand like time
as your elder brother saunters up the road.
As you flex the gut of the string –
ticklish, appraise its elasticity – there stands,
lined up behind you, a frothing cavalry
of years: with iron on their feet, sour
steel against their tongues they are straining
for the order; should the arrow hit the air
they will shoot forth violently and in the time-
honoured fashion as a body.

You do not know them, but the year
depression's dull whisper sends your brother
thump-thudding into silence stands
sweating on the pavement at your rear,
and one is rattling great sleek loops
of motorway on its armoured sides,
the demolition balls which will smash like sugar
your house, your bed, your street, as the truck's
grille smashes through your brother, the tumour
like a stone dents the tender wall of his mind.

As you eye up gleefully the pointed metal tip
of the unbelievably real if truncated arrow
you cannot hear their frenzied neighing
nor feel the ground beneath your small feet slip.
You are a boy of seven, larking about.
All you feel is a flood of whimsy.
Into the new underpass comes water
surging, waves like the manes of horses...
You draw the arrow back like it's a dare,
shoot smartly down a street that doesn't exist.

# In the Annum

In the annum of the weather,
of Anderson [&] McAuley, of the linen store,
of wind flinging itself, like
an illegal logger on the scent of mahogany,
ceaselessly along Royal Avenue's brittle core;
in the annum of the occupants before
the occupants before the
   Annunciation of Tesco;
in the annum.
     In the annum when the public chose
as its favoured means of adornment of the *civitas*
and bird murder
the malleable beauty of plastic, flung
with a gay abandon in its various forms
this to the wind like a logger seeking mahogany;
when the river choired solemnly
a symphony of plastic,
   accompanied by bellows and drums;
in the annum.
     In the annum of the water bomb,
of dog turds crusted on the street
and *The Key to the Kingdom*;
in the annum of the girl's shoe with
a key in the heel and of Loyd Grossman's *Through the Keyhole*,
of the lough's coagulate scum;
in the annum of the one known homeless one,
of five lighters for a pound,
the annum of the underground melody.

    In the annum that preceded
*American Beauty*, in the annum of the ultrasound
of the city, in the annum of the wind

that stung like an illegal logger sniffing out mahogany
through the packed straits of the forest like a disease
and strummed to the river's choked threnody
and passed the party
where a child won shoes with keys in the heel
to ploy with the fingers of the one known homeless one;

                    in the annum of the Kingdom Come
where dirt-fouled fingers ran like birds
in the loft of the brain
up and down the throat of a whistle – a clutch
of green-tipped metal in the hands
of the homeless one –
as senseless and absolute as rain;
in the annum of the end
of the end of days
though scarcely recognised as such
the unknown herald brought to them a different voice.

# Abandoned Asylum

Walking here is like walking the vacated spaces
of your own life: someone should be flitting
in a white gown through the corridors, someone
should be picking the depleted paintwork.

In each glass-fronted private room ought to be a mind
hard-clothed in exile, in exile and resistance;
against the starched garb and the rubber squeak
of the matron, pinked lips ought to be set.

In the woods, somebody, walking alone,
should depict with deliberate, futile steps
their hatred of the calm to be offered up boldly
to the broken – this greenery-slap of health –

and the gleam of the delicate golden plait
washed freshly and affixed with a ribbon
mirror life running through itself like rope
through the hands of a whaler. Against the birds,

pit-a-pat, should echo warm hands knitting
and unknitting horrors, palms pressed
to an upper window, somebody mouthing Help.
And, keeping himself to himself, the gardener

who each night exits with the sun pinned to his chest.

## Sometimes Nothing

She never did it, the girl you were supposed to meet
in pink slippers and dressing gown
in what seemed the dead of night
after the world had gone to bed.

Sodium lights still garnished
the suburban street
with the gladsome hue of territory.
You waited on the curve of the road.
There was nothing in particular to see.

In what claimed to be the dead of night
you stood alone
at the mouth of her development;
sodium lights still salad-dressed the street. What

were you waiting for?
You'd always known she wouldn't do it.
You leaned flimsily
against the curve of the road

where the remnants of a wood
you'd never had the name for scythed
on its cluttered stream
through the new developments,
and no bough juddered in the capricious night.

You stood gilded by the sodium light
as fat forms riffled through
your parents' garden;
you fought to keep yourself concealed
from the nothing that was there.

You wanted to go midnight walking. Where
were you going to walk to?
Through the developments, the pepper sniff of wood?

You, scuffing down the road
in your slippers and your wee fleece dressing gown.
You went home again,
you climbed the creakless stair.
You dreamt the dreams that were appropriate.

## Winter Sunday

Beyond the patio the light drains slowly
from the afternoon's biblical instruction,
the twins fiercely hurling swears
from their gateway as you passed.

Your grandmother may be upstairs
harbouring a soft tang of disinfectant,
or she may be in the cemetery
that is somewhere close by the church on the hill.

Either way she is cold as the animals
whiskering with frost in the beds
and you shut her from your mind
as forcibly as from that mind you banish Jesus.

You watch *The Chronicles of Narnia*
and you wait for your dinner
to the radiator's warm gurgle and click.
Outside, the roses pass singly into the dark.

# Holograph

Loose-legged, baggy-reined, you go
on the mare filled out with summer fatness;
you descend
onto the path by Mitchell's Lake.
It is probable that you smoke.

The tank lurks
under the glitter, to your left,
of lake water,
like a tickle in its throat.
The frogs fang forth,
adobe mysteries.

You hum the rhythm of your way
as the heron
like death's arm launches
from the reaches of the foliage.
It will show itself thus again and again,
and you will always be surprised.

The dark mare flickers
before your eyes,
the scimitar of track withdraws.
Loose-legged, you descend
onto the path by Mitchell's Lake.

# Person

When we ate salt you were uncontrollable a locked-in pony with a lick hiking up those minerals everything had salt added to it not that there was much of anything but still Philadelphia on toast

I don't think you even liked it it was more a proposition a command of earth as we went bone thin as the brittle form clattered across the pavements jinked through the meadows

Our mother said it was a sin how you lived you are taking years off my life she told you when she dug bagged dinners from the satchel we would go out walking you were only ever interested in scouting bins

It's not as though I didn't care you were killing her you sensed fat shaking at my back genuinely caught its ripple as I broached each step though there wasn't any there in the mirror you observed an Alice

But nothing can be claimed self-evident or true to a chemical or the host of one you would eat dry tuna out of cat bowls you would suck salt from an empty plate we were made of chocolate

You measured everything by weight not even weight the size when a hypnotist assayed you you were stout as a pachyderm the fly grey matter redistributed itself in a rhino hide of deflection

Albeit yes a charlatan, deceit leaked off him I could smell it like a horse scents water on the wind it was rank and elemental in his slick suit pocket was the clichéd narrative he'd align you with

Would use no matter what was said just as salt pushed out its
tentacles like the lost tide lapping at a headland as the granite
holds itself and refuses that commingling here is a sprig of
heather, a flower who made it out of this?

# In the Recliner

In the recliner where your two cats sampled suicide
at a five year interval, the first curling himself
fretfully in the narrow gap between the springs and the boards,
the second thrusting his head in the gibbet
of a loose elastic, and where your father took his short-
lived stand on a person's right to keep their own things,
matching or not, which he chose
as his riot shield against the endlessly new,
the red line that she couldn't cross (she crossed it) –
no, you can't remember what you did there.
Sat, probably, taking account of nothing, crisp or moot.

# Madeleine

Applying a dollop of NAF *Pimp My Pony*, pink as Love Hearts or as bubblegum, to the bottom of the wide wash bucket; frothing water from the hose, thrusting in the brush and then the shit-tasselled tail, you are expecting, as you swirl, dissolved stick sugar to envelop the behind of the animal you're lathering in nine pound luxuries deployed, the label is ecstatic to declare, by —— and ——; anticipating candy floss, the queue for the Waltzer, you do that freakish thing with your nostrils – you can close them off without needing to touch – then open up and tilt clear channels for the punch of the exquisitely ersatz upon that rough, wintery hide.

Sly, blushingly consumable, what fans from the scrubbed hind-quarters is the actual smelltrack of your summers: the stuff your father used to slosh around the portaloo at the cottage in Down. Rain's blowing in from the sea; you have him there, a moment, wrestling the bog to the copse – and parallel to that you're thinking Carl Hester uses this... How odd... Or was it Charlotte Dujardin – then someone comes wanting the hose and you have to stop standing like a meerkat on alert, you have to uncrinkle; you grab the dripping shaft of the mare's tail, spin it till she's almost lifting off.

# IndyRef, 2014

You are like the mare who won't
ford streams but will only jump them,
refusing and refusing,
churning up the ground as,
under, the stones wink silver
or is it rust. Do not
raise a stick to her,
for this is how you board boats
steaming out of harbour,
stitching the Irish Sea
with the needlework of narrative
that snips up short.
And how you vote,
and how you ride her: for months
paralysis, then thinking Ah
fuck it what's the worst
that could happen Jump. And
Yes, you mark the ballot, Yes.
The puddles glimmer,
you could put your foot
right through them to Australia.
On Staffa, the long
lost granite columns moan.

# Samhain

Who do you propitiate, whose altar the makeshift hull
into which you pitch, as Tigernmas pitched the skull
of a first born infant annually into rock
by way of diverting the malevolence of Crom Cruach,
not just the propinquities of the passing year
but your whole life up until this point, in yellowed paper.

Much of it is as thin as the veil between existences;
on much, the once-strong evidence is fading to a hiss,
illegible as ash. The numerals are out of date,
it's long since anyone could thus strip you of your assets,
yet you still tear viciously at every last receipt
and quarter the identifying heart. The room is neat,

neat like you've never had anything in all your time,
and in the purifying snows is a kind of satisfaction.
Witherwards, its face carved out of open air,
whatever you have served smirks gauntly back at Lúnasa –
remarks the leaves still folded stiffly in the table,
the mountains of salt in which you have drowned your meal.

# Moths

Something changed when I wasn't looking:
*gies* and *cannae* came like moths to test their wings
on the filament of my tongue;
when we moved we discovered small moths
had been steadily eating through my fabrics.

And although you, chivalric with the Dyson,
like an anteater manfully sucked them up,
they slipped the plastic bin.
There is one already in the ottoman
mustering fresh reserves, battening upon my tights.

Grain locusts of my heart, my *ding an sich*!
In your painting of the Old Man of Storr
the diaphanous scrim of my breasts overlays him.

I am hovering in stonewash blue, I am stamped
on the image like a pale moth on a pale tree,
a white crow on a field of white, or nearly.

# NOTES

**Wonderland** (15)

'Wonderland' is in memory of Bijan Ebrahimi.

**Betty Staff's** (26)

Betty, twice all-Ireland ballroom champion and proprietor of a studio in the Entries off Ann Street in central Belfast, was my maternal grandmother.

**The Canal at Fountainbridge** (50) and **Moths** (74)

Along with 'IndyRef, 2014' (72), these poems were written in collaborative conversation with poems by Nerys Williams and were originally included in the co-authored pamphlet *City of Two Suns* (part of the Irish Writers' Centre's 'Compass Lines' project). Nerys is Welsh and lives in Dublin; I am Northern Irish and live in Edinburgh. Among other things, we were interested in attempting to explore displacement without nostalgia.

'Moths' makes reference to a white crow, which derives from an image in one of Nerys's poems: Nerys's piece centres on Branwen, miserable exile in Ireland and the literal translation of whose name into English is 'white crow'. The history of the peppered moth, which features in both 'Moths' and 'The Canal at Fountainbridge', is a prominent example of unintended human interference in species evolution: the relative success of the two forms of the moth fluctuated dramatically during and after the Industrial Revolution.

**Little Monument: Se Vende** (54)

The Museo del Mar 'Las Caracoles' housed the personal collection of José María Garrido; the city council of Sanlúcar de Barrameda did not much care for it, or him. Further information at http://spacesarchives.org/explore/collection/environment/jose-maria-garrido-/

**Samhain** (73)

During Samhain – a liminal time at which the boundaries between worlds are abnormally traversable – salt was traditionally carried to ward off spirits.

MIX
Paper from
responsible sources
FSC® C007785